# Hilarious ONE- LINERS

## GENE PERRET
## WITH TERRY PERRET MARTIN

Illustrated by Myron Miller

**Sterling Publishing Co., Inc.  New York**

Edited by Jeanette Green

**Library of Congress Cataloging-in-Publication Data**

Hilarious one-liners / by Gene Perret ; with Terry Perret Martin ;
illustrated by Myron Miller.
    p.    cm.
    Includes index.
    ISBN 0-8069-1352-5
    1. Quotations, English.   2. American wit and humor.   I. Perret,
Gene.   II. Martin, Terry Perret.
PN6081.H45   1996
081—dc20                                      95-39432

3   5   7   9   10   8   6   4   2

Published by Sterling Publishing Company, Inc.
387 Park Avenue South, New York, N.Y. 10016
© 1996 by Gene Perret and Terry Perret Martin
Distributed in Canada by Sterling Publishing
℅ Canadian Manda Group, One Atlantic Avenue, Suite 105
Toronto, Ontario, Canada M6K 3E7
Distributed in Great Britain and Europe by Cassell PLC
Wellington House, 125 Strand, London WC2R 0BB, England
Distributed in Australia by Capricorn Link (Australia) Pty Ltd.
P.O. Box 6651, Baulkham Hills, Business Centre, NSW 2153, Australia
*Manufactured in the United States of America*

Sterling ISBN 0-8069-1352-5

# CONTENTS

# DEDICATIONS

To Martha Bolton,
a cherished co-writer
and an awesome writing competitor
*—Gene*

To my Colorado family
*—Terry*

**The early bird would never catch the worm
if the dumb worm slept late.**
                                        —*Milton Berle*

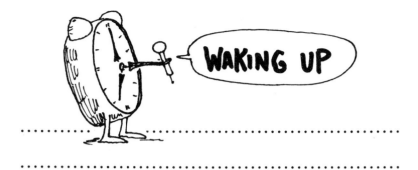

You should see the way my wife looks in the morning. She ran after the garbage man and said, "Am I too late for the garbage?" He said, "No, jump in." —*Henny Youngman*

I tried giving up coffee in the morning, but I noticed something. When I woke up, I didn't. —*Milton Berle*

If your eyes hurt after you drink coffee in the morning, you have to take the spoon out of the cup. —*Norm Crosby*

Nowadays I'm beginning to have morning sickness. I'm not having a baby—it's just that I'm sick of morning. —*Phyllis Diller*

Men are very strange. When they wake up in the morning they want things like toast. I don't have these recipes. —*Elayne Boosler*

Last week I noticed my gums were shrinking. I was brushing my teeth with Preparation H. —*Rodney Dangerfield*

★ ★ ★ ★ ★

There is no such thing as a good morning. They all begin with waking up.

—— ★ ——

I must look a mess when I get up. My wife hires a woman to come in once a day and kiss me good morning.

—— ★ ——

I look so awful when I get up in the morning, I have the mirror inside the medicine chest.

—— ★ ——

Some people hate waking up and getting out of bed. I enjoy it. I do it three or four times a day.

—— ★ ——

There are 24 hours in a day. Do you realize if there were 24 hours and 15 minutes we could all get enough sleep?

—— ★ ——

For me, there's one good thing about waking up in the morning—the realization that everything I do for the rest of the day is going to be easier than this.

—— ★ ——

My mother always used to tell me that the early bird catches the worm. It's probably one of the least appealing incentives for getting out of bed I've ever heard.

. . . If I get out of bed early, I want a better reward than a slimy worm.

—— ★ ——

I hate to get up in the morning. I like to climb into my water bed and stay there as long as the water does.

—— ★ ——

My wife said I can have breakfast in bed anytime I want it. All I have to do is sleep in the kitchen.

—— ★ ——

The first thing I do when I get up in the morning is jump in the shower. Someday I'm going to learn to take my pajamas off first.

—— ★ ——

My uncle was a farmer and he only slept late one day in his life—the day the rooster had laryngitis.

—— ★ ——

In England, people actually try to be brilliant at breakfast. Only dull people are brilliant at breakfast.  —*Oscar Wilde*

Our toaster works on either AC or DC, but not on bread. It has two settings—too soon or too late.  —*Sam Levenson*

Never work before breakfast. If you have to work before breakfast, eat your breakfast first.  —*Josh Billings*

Breakfast cereals that come in the same colors as polyester leisure suits make oversleeping a virtue.  —*Fran Lebowitz*

★　　★　　★　　★　　★

At my house I enjoy breakfast the most. At the other meals I'm awake enough to know what the food is.

—— ★ ——

I'm too lazy to make breakfast. I just give the family slices of bread and call it Toast Tartare.

—— ★ ——

I'm amazed at people who eat a big breakfast. How can you work up an appetite sleeping?

—— ★ ——

I love the smell of fresh coffee in the morning. That's why I use Maxwell House After-Shave Lotion.

—— ★ ——

I think if I have a good breakfast I could go without food for the rest of the day. I think that until about lunchtime.

—— ★ ——

I don't like cereal that snaps, crackles, and pops in the morning. I want it to be like me—just sit there and sop up the milk.

—— ★ ——

I went to a restaurant where three eggs cost $8.95. The waitress said, "Would you like them scrambled?" I said, "No. At $3 an egg I want to count them."

—— ★ ——

Brunch is a meal somewhere between breakfast and lunch. What would you call a meal you have somewhere around three in the morning? A midnight sneakfast?

—— ★ ——

I am a total animal until I've had my first cup of coffee in the morning. If coffee had never been invented, I could have been Jack-the-Ripper.

—— ★ ——

My wife always burns the toast and leaves the eggs runny. I said, "Tomorrow morning why don't you scramble the bread and pop the eggs in the toaster?"

—— ★ ——

I served my wife breakfast in bed the other day. She enjoyed it, then spent the rest of the day cleaning up the kitchen.

—— ★ ——

Half the people like to work and the other half don't, or maybe it's the other way around.                    —*Sam Levenson*

Anyone can do any amount of work, provided it isn't the work he is supposed to be doing at that moment.

—*Robert Benchley*

It is better to have a permanent income than to be fascinating.

—*Oscar Wilde*

The man with the best job in the country is the Vice President. All he has to do is get up every morning and say, "How's the President?"

—*Will Rogers*

He works 8 hours a day and sleeps 8 hours a day. The same 8 hours.

—*Milton Berle*

People who work sitting down get paid more than people who work standing up.

—*Ogden Nash*

My brother-in-law has an allergy. He's allergic to work.

—*Henny Youngman*

He's a real workaholic. You mention work, he gets drunk.

—*Rodney Dangerfield*

My brother-in-law worked in a winery stepping on grapes. He got fired one day when they caught him sitting down on the job.

—*Henny Youngman*

I think the easiest job in the world has to be coroner. Surgery on dead people. What's the worst thing that could happen?

—*Dennis Miller*

★ ★ ★ ★ ★

As if getting up in the morning isn't bad enough, it has to be followed by going to work.

—— ★ ——

Getting up and going to work in the morning . . . what a waste of 8 good hours of sleep.

—— ★ ——

I don't mind going to work in the morning. I don't mind coming home, either. It's the 8 hours in between that get my goat.

I have a simple definition of work: anything that has to be done standing up.

I don't like to drink too much coffee in the morning. If I do, I toss and turn all through the work day.

I like driving the crowded freeways to work in the morning. It's a chance to see new faces and learn a lot of new hand signals.

Some people can't wait to get to work on Monday morning. They're the ones who won the football pool over the weekend.

Some experts claim work can be fun if you make a game of it. So I did—hide-and-seek.

. . . I don't show up at the office, and they have to come find me.

The 24-hour day works out perfectly. We get 8 hours for sleep, 8 hours for work, and 8 hours to complain about too much work and not enough sleep.

The first thing I do when I get to the office is have a cup of coffee before getting down to serious work. —Which convinces me that what this country really needs is a good 8-hour cup of coffee.

The only good thing about going to work is that it's a prerequisite to coming home from work.

## SOME ODD JOBS

One of my first office jobs was cleaning the windows on the envelopes.                                        —*Rita Rudner*

For a while I had a series of very unusual jobs. I was a night watchman in a day camp, a deckhand on a submarine, a traffic director in a phone booth, and a cruise director on a Ferris wheel.                  —*Jackie Vernon*

I used to be a translator for bad mimes.   —*Steven Wright*

He was a falsie manufacturer. He lived off the flat of the land.                                           —*Groucho Marx*

My brother-in-law just got a job as a lifeguard in a car wash.                                            —*Henny Youngman*

I used to be a proofreader for a skywriting company.
                                                      —*Steven Wright*

★　★　★　★　★

**The amount of sleep required by the average person is about 5 minutes longer.**
**—Max Kauffmann**

Any kid will run any errand for you, if you ask at bedtime.
—*Red Skelton*

My wife came to bed one night with her hair in curlers and grease on her face. I didn't know whether to kiss her or play trick-or-treat. —*Slappy White*

The only thing he ever takes out on a moonlit night is his upper plate. —*Fred Allen*

When my wife goes to sleep at night, she packs so much mud on her face, I say, "Good night, swamp!"
—*Henny Youngman*

It's true Fang and I fight, but we've never gone to bed mad. Of course, one year we were up for 3 months.
—*Phyllis Diller*

Do you know what it means to come home at night to a woman who'll give you a little love, a little affection, a little tenderness? It means you're in the wrong house, that's what it means. —*Henny Youngman*

I hate it when my foot falls asleep during the day—because then I know it will be up all night. —*Steven Wright*

★   ★   ★   ★   ★

Bedtime is not my favorite time of the day. It comes right before my favorite time of the day.

—— ★ ——

My kid is very good about kissing me goodnight and going up to bed without a fuss. He should be. He does it three, four, five times a night.

—— ★ ——

For a long time I couldn't close my eyes at night to get to sleep. My wife finally figured out the problem—the drawstring on my pajamas was too tight.

—— ★ ——

My wife's mad at me because I went to sleep early last night. About 12 feet before I got to the front door.

—— ★ ——

My wife and I always kiss goodnight. It's like touching gloves before we spend the entire night fighting over the covers.

—— ★ ——

I'm not really good at math, but I have trouble figuring out why my better half requires three-fourths of the covers at night.

—— ★ ——

Every night, when I go to bed, I kiss my wife good night and my covers good-bye.

—— ★ ——

My wife always steals my covers during the night. What bothers me most about this is that we have twin beds.

—— ★ ——

My wife says, "Why do you have to go to sleep so early every night?" I say, "I'm anxious to dream about you."

—— ★ ——

My wife and I always settle any disagreements before going to bed at night. Then we try to fall asleep real fast before the next fight starts.

—— ★ ——

I always set my alarm before going to bed at night. It gives me something to ignore in the morning.

—— ★ ——

My uncle invented a coffee that makes you see double. If it keeps you up at night, you'll have company.

—— ★ ——

I woke up and my girl asked if I slept good. I said, "No, I made a couple of mistakes."　　　　　　　—*Steven Wright*

I have never taken any exercise—except sleep and rest.
　　　　　　　　　　　　　　　　　　　　—*Mark Twain*

I bought one of those tapes to teach you Spanish in your sleep. During the night, the record skipped. The next day I could only stutter in Spanish.　　　　—*Steven Wright*

My wife missed her nap today. Slept right through it.
　　　　　　　　　　　　　　　　　　—*Henny Youngman*

I just passed the age of 30, and you get a little introspective once you pass 30. Like I'm beginning to appreciate the value of a nap.　　　　　　　　　　—*Marsha Warfield*

Can you remember when you didn't want to sleep? Isn't it inconceivable? I guess the definition of adulthood is that you want to sleep.　　　　　　　　—*Paula Poundstone*

★　★　★　★　★

I don't think humans were meant to walk upright—because it tires me out so quickly.

—— ★ ——

Sleep is probably the most fun you can have in this life without being awake to enjoy it.

—— ★ ——

I sleep a lot. The only exercise I get is tossing and turning.

—— ★ ——

The only way sleep could be more enjoyable for me is if I could find a way to make money from it.

—— ★ ——

My hobby is napping. It's not only fun, but inexpensive.

—— ★ ——

Some people say they can't sleep at night. That may be true, although I've never been awake to hear them say it.

—— ★ ——

I love sleep. To me, anything done with both eyes open already has two strikes against it.

—— ★ ——

Horses can sleep standing up. Of course, if you pulled a milk wagon all day, you probably could, too.

—— ★ ——

Do you know what I call people who get 8 hours' sleep a night? Amateurs.

—— ★ ——

Sharks never sleep. That's why you'll never catch one wearing pajamas.

—— ★ ——

Sleep is meant to refresh, rejuvenate, and revitalize us, so we'll be ready for another good night's sleep tomorrow night.

—— ★ ——

I do a lot of sleeping. When I was married, I asked the Sandman to be my best man.

—— ★ ——

Sleep is nature's way of saying, "Ssshhh."

—— ★ ——

I had a terrible dream yesterday. I dreamed I was awake all night. —*Milton Berle*

This morning I woke up from a dream and went right into a daydream. —*Steven Wright*

He dreamed he was eating shredded wheat and woke up to find the mattress half gone. —*Fred Allen*

You know a man is getting old when his dreams about girls are reruns. —*Henny Youngman*

My aunt said to her husband, "Max, last night I dreamed you bought me a fur coat." Her husband said, "In your next dream, wear it in good health." —*Henny Youngman*

I just had a wonderful dream. I dreamed the Joneses were trying to keep up with *me*. —*Henny Youngman*

I had a terrible dream last night. I dreamed that my girl and Sophia Loren had a fight over me. And my girl won. —*Joe E. Lewis*

★ ★ ★ ★ ★

A little boy asked his friend, "How old are you?" The friend said, "I don't know. Four or five." The older boy asked, "Do you dream about girls?" The friend said, "No." The boy said, "You're four."

—— ★ ——

**19**

One thing I like about dreams: you have to be asleep to have them.

———— ★ ————

Dreams are like sermons in church. They're better if you sleep right through them.

———— ★ ————

I was having such a terrible dream the other night that it woke me up. Then I realized my real life was worse.

———— ★ ————

I dreamed I was stuck on a deserted island with three gorgeous women. The sad part was, I was a palm tree.

———— ★ ————

My wife woke me last night and said, "I'm having a terrible dream." I said, "Ask for your money back."

———— ★ ————

Last week I dreamed the entire night that I was running from people who were chasing me. When I woke up, I was not only covered with perspiration, but I was somewhere in Ohio.

———— ★ ————

I think I watch too much television. Last night, my dreams kept being interrupted for commercials.

———— ★ ————

I do watch too much TV. I had a dream the other night, and at the end of it, a list of credits rolled by.

———— ★ ————

Television has definitely influenced me. I'm searching now for a stand-up comedian to star in my dreams.

———— ★ ————

The other night I dreamed I was a Boy Scout who won a knot-tying contest. When I woke up I couldn't get the drawstring on my pajamas undone.

———— ★ ————

The other night I dreamed I was a shark who swam in oceans all over the world. When I woke up, boy, were my gills tired.

—— ★ ——

I dreamed the other night that I was a soldier in Custer's last stand. When I woke up my pajamas were at half-mast.

—— ★ ——

There ain't no way to find out why a snorer can't hear himself snore.
—*Mark Twain*

★　★　★　★　★

My spouse snores so loudly, the people in my dreams complain that they can't hear one another talk.

—— ★ ——

My husband says, "How can you prove that I snore so loudly?" I say, "Look, those windows weren't broken when we went to bed last night."

—— ★ ——

Snoring is nature's way of saying, "Hey, everybody wake up and look at me. I'm sleeping."

—— ★ ——

My husband snores so loudly I think he studied sleeping under Harley-Davidson.

—— ★ ——

There's only one sure cure for snoring: insomnia.

—— ★ ——

My husband's snoring is not always so bad. Sometimes it drowns out the noise of passing trains.

—— ★ ——

I've discovered that a glass of cool water can stop my husband's snoring—if I pour it down the front of his pajamas.

—— ★ ——

Some scientists say a tennis ball sewn into the back of the pajamas can stop snoring. I'd rather just whack the snorer on the head with the racket.

—— ★ ——

My husband's snoring is so bad we have to sleep in shifts. I try to sneak in a nap while he's inhaling.

—— ★ ——

My husband's snoring saves me a fortune in beauty treatments. He snores so loud it curls my hair.

. . . And my toes.

—— ★ ——

My husband's snoring sounds like the mating call of the elephant seal. Every morning he gets love letters from the Pacific Ocean.

—— ★ ——

A good cure for insomnia is: Get plenty of sleep.
—*W. C. Fields*

Don't wake him up. He's got insomnia. He's trying to sleep
it off.                                          —*Chico Marx*

Life is something that happens when you can't get to sleep.
—*Fran Lebowitz*

★   ★   ★   ★   ★

The doctor says I might have insomnia, but I'm not going
to lose any sleep over it.

—— ★ ——

I wish someone would find a cure for my insomnia. I
dreamed about that all last night.

—— ★ ——

My uncle hasn't slept a wink in about three years. He's a
great guy to buy used pajamas from.

—— ★ ——

My uncle has a very bad case of insomnia. He goes to flop
houses and then can't flop.

—— ★ ——

My uncle's under a lot of stress because of medical reasons.
He has insomnia and sleeping sickness at the same time.

—— ★ ——

Uncle:   I've got amnesia so bad I haven't slept in 5 weeks.
Me:   No, Uncle. *Insomnia* is when you can't sleep.
Uncle:   Oh, I *can* sleep. I just keep forgetting to.

—— ★ ——

The good news is that my uncle finally got over his insomnia. The bad news is that he was driving on the interstate
at the time.

—— ★ ——

I had an appointment with a doctor who promised he
could cure my insomnia, but he overslept.

—— ★ ——

Look at the bright side of insomnia—it's a great cure for snoring.

—— ★ ——

My doctor can't cure my insomnia, but he does the next best thing. He tells me how well he slept.

—— ★ ——

I think I might be getting over my insomnia. The other day my foot fell asleep.

—— ★ ——

I've had insomnia for 7 weeks and finally last night I fell asleep. My wife woke me up to tell me the good news.

—— ★ ——

There are some advantages to having insomnia. Now I know when my husband is stealing the covers.

—— ★ ——

We do more talking progress than
we do progressing.

—*Will Rogers*

**PROGRESS**

Happiness and contentment is progress. In fact that's all progress is. —*Will Rogers*

Things ain't what they used to be; in fact, at our house, they never was. —*Herb Shriner*

It's hard to get used to these changing times. I can remember when the air was clean and the sex was dirty. —*George Burns*

George: Gracie, what do you think of television?
Gracie: I think it's wonderful. I hardly ever watch radio anymore. —*George Burns and Gracie Allen*

When I was a boy of 14, my father was so ignorant. But when I got to be 21, I was amazed to see how much he had learned in seven years. —*Mark Twain*

The old believe everything; the middle-aged suspect everything; the young know everything. —*Oscar Wilde*

Progress might have been all right once but it has gone on far too long. —*Ogden Nash*

How times have changed! Remember 30 years ago when a juvenile delinquent was a kid with an overdue library book? —*Henny Youngman*

★ ★ ★ ★ ★

If things keep getting better all the time, how come so many people remember the "good old days"?

———— ★ ————

Progress sometimes means we just have a faster way of doing something that was never necessary in the first place.

———— ★ ————

I hate progress. It means that everything improves over time except me.

———— ★ ————

Progress is not always good. I remember when moving pictures started talking. Now the entire audience does, too.

———— ★ ————

Progress means just when we can afford something, they make a new and better one that we can't.

———— ★ ————

They had pollution in the old days, but at least you could put it on your roses.

———— ★ ————

Have you noticed? Everything in the world keeps improving except people.

———— ★ ————

Cars can now go five times as fast as they used to, but there are twenty times more of them, so, it takes twice as long to get there.

———— ★ ————

One of the many things that hasn't improved with technology is conversation.

———— ★ ————

Because of progress we all now own a toaster where the bread pops up when it's burnt.

———— ★ ————

Is it progress when we have coffee that won't keep us awake at night and television shows that won't either?

———— ★ ————

## MODERN TECHNOLOGY

We got a new garbage disposal—my brother-in-law. He'll eat anything.　　　　　　　　　　　*—Henny Youngman*

With today's technology, they have artificial replacements for everything. You don't have to worry about getting old; you have to worry about rusting.　　　　　*—George Burns*

My father was replaced at work with a gadget that's about this big that does everything my father does, but better. The depressing thing is my mother went out and bought one.　　　　　　　　　　　　　*—Woody Allen*

Sure my mother had an automatic garbage disposal. She would detect unerringly when you planned to go out, and put the garbage bag in your hand.　　　*—Sam Levenson*

Freezing people for the future isn't a new idea; landlords discovered it years ago.　　　　　　　*—Pat Cooper*

The Concorde travels at twice the speed of sound, which is fun, except that you can't hear the movie until 2 hours after you land.　　　　　　　　　*—Howie Mandel*

I flew over on the Concorde. That plane is so fast it gives you an extra couple of hours to look for your luggage.
　　　　　　　　　　　　　　*—Bob Hope*

America is angry that we lost our technological edge. But we're not a scientific country anymore; think about it: We couldn't even go metric.　　　　　　*—Bill Maher*

With today's technology, flying is much faster. To give you an idea of how fast we traveled: When we left we had two rabbits, and when we got there, we still had only two.
—*Bob Hope*

My new car is so modern you press a button and *it* presses a button.                                      —*Henny Youngman*

★   ★   ★   ★   ★


The world is getting too technologically advanced. I was just talking about that with my clone the other day. . . .

—— ★ ——

My uncle has had every part of his body replaced. He's still alive, but hardly anybody recognizes him.

—— ★ ——

Everything today is done by machines. The world is not going to come to an end. It's just going to sit around a long time waiting for the repairman.

—— ★ ——

Technology is moving so fast nowadays it's tough on scientists. By the time you invent anything today it has already become obsolete.

—— ★ ——

They've improved practically everything on television, except the programming.

—— ★ ——

We're doing a lot of things today that we shouldn't be doing—just because we can.

. . . And some things that aren't even worth doing, we're doing more quickly.

—— ★ ——

Technology has its drawbacks. I've yet to meet an Indian who couldn't send a smoke signal because of a power blackout.

—— ★ ——

**29**

I often wonder: where did people hang their children's drawings before the refrigerator was invented?

—— ★ ——

There's only one thing left for science to invent: something useful that doesn't beep or flash.

—— ★ ——

You know, it's a shame the big bang didn't happen at this moment in time. We could have videotaped it.

—— ★ ——

Every form of communication has been vastly improved by modern technology, except conversation.

—— ★ ——

Man, endowed with that incredible computer known as the human brain, has used it to invent an electronic brain.
—*Sam Levenson*

The computer didn't eliminate red tape; it only perforated it. —*Sam Levenson*

They finally came up with the perfect office computer. If it makes a mistake, it blames another computer.
—*Milton Berle*

I hate computers. When I went to school, all I had was a pencil and the kid next to me. . . . And I think if he had applied himself, I could have been somebody.
—*Allen Stephan*

★   ★   ★   ★   ★

Computers used to be user-friendly. Now they're getting downright flirtatious.

—— ★ ——

Computers are fast. I can now make ten times the mistakes I used to make manually.

—— ★ ——

Just think, if Shakespeare had had a computer, he probably would have accidentally erased *A Midsummer Night's Dream*.

... And *Troilus and Cressida* would have been kicked out the first time he ran through the spell-check.

—— ★ ——

Remember, computers can't think for themselves. They're just like any other worker in your office.

—— ★ ——

Since the introduction of computers into the workplace, I'm now the second smartest thing sitting at my desk.

—— ★ ——

With computers we can now do a full-day's work in 1 hour. Of course, it takes us 7 hours to figure out what we did.

—— ★ ——

My computer was acting strangely, but the repairman figured out what the problem was. He said there was a nut loose at the keyboard.

—— ★ ——

Computers are not intelligent. If they were, they wouldn't let us humans anywhere near them.

—— ★ ——

They say computers can't think, but I have one that does. It thinks it's broken.

—— ★ ——

I bought a new program that helps me figure out my family budget. First thing it figured out was that I couldn't afford this program.

—— ★ ——

With the computer I still do dumb things, but now I can list them in either alphabetical or chronological order.

—— ★ ——

The computer is a poor substitute for intelligence, but then, aren't we all?

—— ★ ——

There's so much romance in Paris, the storks have to wear beepers.
—*Bob Hope*

★　　★　　★　　★　　★

My boss wanted me to wear a beeper but I refused. I don't want anything else on my body that could fall off.

—— ★ ——

My boss said, "I want to be able to reach you no matter where you travel." I said, "Then come with me."

". . . You can drive."

—— ★ ——

I don't like beepers. If I have strange noises coming from my body unexpectedly, I want it to mean I have indigestion.

—— ★ ——

I put the wrong size of batteries in the beeper that I wear on my belt. The first call I got blew my shoes off.

—— ★ ——

My beeper went off in the middle of the opera. Four of the spear carriers threw them at me.

—— ★ ——

I have a terrible job—important enough for a beeper but not important enough for a raise.

—— ★ ——

A friend of mine is very cheap. His beeper is on a party line.

—— ★ ——

I think my beeper is a little too powerful. Every time I get a message, my garage door opens.

—— ★ ——

One advertisement said, "Get a beeper and never miss an important call." I just sit by the phone and I never miss not having a beeper.

—— ★ ——

My dog has a special beeper. He knows which dogs are in heat over a five-state area.

—— ★ ——

My secretary called me on my beeper to tell me that I left my beeper in the office.

—— ★ ——

ANSWERING MACHINES

I hate those answering machines which advise me in a 30-second prerecorded speech that I will have 10 seconds to talk when I hear the beep in 5 seconds.
—*Sam Levenson*

I like to leave a message before the beep. —*Steven Wright*

★   ★   ★   ★   ★

People are living longer nowadays because when the Angel of Death calls, he generally gets an answering machine.

—— ★ ——

People are getting used to answering machines. I called and got a real person last week and neither one of us spoke. We were both waiting for the beep.

—— ★ ——

Everybody's got them. My grandparents bought an answering machine and they don't even have a phone.

—— ★ ——

Have you ever noticed? Everytime you return the calls on your answering machine, you get their answering machine.

—— ★ ——

I have a very devious answering machine. It says, "Please leave your message after the beep." . . . And then there is no beep.

It saves me a fortune in return phone calls.

—— ★ ——

My brother and I haven't spoken to each other in 2 years. We're not having a fight; that's when we both got answering machines.

—— ★ ——

A friend of mine has an honest message on his answering machine. It says, "I'm home right now but I don't feel like talking to you. Please leave a message and I'll call you back when you don't feel like talking to me."

—— ★ ——

I climbed a mountain and hollered "Helloooo." A voice came back that said, "The echo is busy at the moment. Leave a message at the beep, and we'll get back to you as soon as possible."

—— ★ ——

You get home now and get all the messages on your answering machine. It's the electronic version of junk mail.

—— ★ ——

At home, I have a map of the United States
—actual size. I spent all last summer
folding it.

—*Steven Wright*

**PATRIOTISM**

It will take America two more wars to learn the words to our national anthem.          —*Will Rogers*

It is a point of pride for the American male to keep the same size Jockey shorts for his entire life.     —*Bill Cosby*

I have an American Legion dog. He stops at every post.
                                                        —*Milton Berle*

Whenever you hear a man speak of his love for his country, it is a sign that he expects to be paid for it.
                                                        —*H. L. Mencken*

"Oh, give me a home where the buffalo roam, . . ." and I'll show you a house full of dirt.          —*Marty Allen*

I'm still recovering from a shock. I was nearly drafted. It's not that I mind fighting for my country, but they called me at a ridiculous time: in the middle of a war.
                                                        —*Jackie Mason*

A yuppie wouldn't salute the flag if it wasn't 100% cotton.
                                                        —*Mark Russell*

America is the only country where you can go on the air and kid politicians—and where politicians go on the air and kid the people.          —*Groucho Marx*

★   ★   ★   ★   ★

Ask not what your country can do for you, but how much it's going to cost you for them to do it.

—— ★ ——

I love God and country in that order . . . because God doesn't charge taxes.

—— ★ ——

My uncle is a great patriot, but he's also very lazy. His goal in life is to write a national anthem that we can all sit down to.

—— ★ ——

My uncle says that America is the only country that he would ever live in. It's not that he's a patriot; his passport has been taken away from him.

—— ★ ——

I have an uncle who is very proud of the fact that he has never voted for any politician. He says, "It only encourages them."

—— ★ ——

I have another uncle who says that America is the most beautiful land he's ever seen in the entire country.

—— ★ ——

My other uncle hates taxes. When they play the national anthem, he puts his hand over his wallet.

—— ★ ——

My uncle is a great patriot. He says he loves all 48 states. His heart is big, but his geography book is terribly outdated.

—— ★ ——

I have a friend who is a California kid at heart, but he happens to live in Kansas. His ambition is to someday go surfing on the amber waves of grain.

—— ★ ——

I have one question: If America is filled with amber waves of grain, how come cereal costs so much?

—— ★ ——

I have an uncle who is a great patriot but a lousy judge of tattoo artists. He has a tattoo over his chest that reads, "*E pluribus unub.*"

—— ★ ——

# LIFE, LIBERTY & THE PURSUIT OF HAPPINESS

Liberty don't work as good in practice as it does in speech.
—*Will Rogers*

Liberty means responsibility. That is why most men dread it. —*George Bernard Shaw*

A husband is a man who lost his liberty in the pursuit of happiness. —*Milton Berle*

Happiness? A good cigar, a good meal, and good woman—or a bad woman. It depends on how much happiness you can handle. —*George Burns*

Money can't buy happiness. It just helps you look for it in more places. —*Milton Berle*

It's pretty hard to tell what does bring happiness; both poverty and wealth have failed. —*Kin Hubbard*

I never knew what real happiness was until I got married. And then it was too late. —*Max Kauffman*

Some people bring happiness wherever they go; you bring happiness *when*ever you go. —*Henny Youngman*

★　★　★　★　★

The most precious thing we have is life. Yet it has absolutely no trade-in value.

—— ★ ——

We all treasure life. In fact, most of us carry it with us to our deathbed.

—— ★ ——

Nathan Hale is famous for saying, "I regret I have but one life to give for my country." His cat made the same speech nine times.　　—— ★ ——

Life is what we do while we're waiting for the other shoe to drop.

—— ★ ——

It's amazing the rights people will give up to be free.

—— ★ ——

Liberty is the right to complain that we don't have enough freedom.

—— ★ ——

Have you ever noticed? The Statue of Liberty is not allowed to move.

—— ★ ——

I've been engaged in the pursuit of happiness all my life. When I got it, I found out I couldn't afford it.

—— ★ ——

We're all free to pursue happiness for as long as we wish—or we can just take a cash settlement.

—— ★ ——

Our constitution guarantees us the right to the pursuit of happiness. Unfortunately, we do have to provide our own funds.

—— ★ ——

Our forefathers guaranteed us the right to the pursuit of happiness. They should have given us a few clues as to where to look.

—— ★ ——

Will I ever attain happiness in this life? If Sharon Stone responds favorably to my letter, I might.

—— ★ ——

**Judge:** Order! Order in the court!
**Defendant:** I'll have a ham sandwich.
—*Milton Berle*

# COURTROOM

When you go to court you are putting your fate into the hands of 12 people who weren't smart enough to get out of jury duty.
                                                    —*Norm Crosby*

A jury consists of 12 persons chosen to decide who has the better lawyer.
                                                    —*Robert Frost*

We have a criminal jury system which is superior to any in the world, and its efficiency is only marred by the difficulty of finding 12 men every day who don't know anything and can't read.
                                                    —*Mark Twain*

I heard that Evelyn Wood just lost a lawsuit. A guy sued because his eyeball blew out at 10,000 words a minute.
                                                    —*Jay Leno*

Lawsuit: A machine you go into as a pig and come out sausage.
                                                    —*Ambrose Bierce*

This woman driver hit a guy and knocked him 6 feet in the air. Then she sued him for leaving the scene of the accident.
                                                    —*Henny Youngman*

★　★　★　★　★

A man said he was going to sue me for everything I owned. I said, "Great, then you can make the payments on it."

—— ★ ——

When I was jury foreman, the judge asked me, "How did you find the defendant?" I said, "He was sitting over there the whole time."

—— ★ ——

I think the judge was slightly biased. He told the jury, "Remember, this criminal is innocent until proven guilty."

——— ★ ———

There was once a movie called *Twelve Angry Men*. It was about Zsa Zsa Gabor's ex-husbands on alimony day.

——— ★ ———

I think I made a fool of myself when they put me on the witness stand. I kept pleading the 5th commandment.

——— ★ ———

I told the judge I was guilty; I was the cat burglar. He sentenced me to nine life sentences.

——— ★ ———

My lawyer said, "You should be glad you were only sentenced to 487 years in prison. You could have gotten life."

I said, "I hope you're better at filing appeals than you are at doing math."

——— ★ ———

You're entitled to a jury of your peers. I tried to get out of jury duty by saying, "I don't know what a peer is and I don't think I've ever been one."

The judge said, "That just means you're somebody's equal." I said, "Then I really should get off. I've never been that either."

——— ★ ———

I was on the jury at a murder trial and I complained to the judge that the chairs were uncomfortable. The defendant said, "You ought to see the one they're trying to put me in."

——— ★ ———

The defendant came into the courtroom wearing a fright wig, a big red nose, and large, floppy shoes. The jury found him legally inane.

——— ★ ———

There's a new law that doesn't allow you to change your clothes on the beach anymore, but that doesn't bother me. I change my clothes on the bus on the way down to the beach. —*Henny Youngman*

I learned law so well, the day I graduated I sued the college, won the case, and got my tuition back. —*Fred Allen*

My parents didn't want to move to Florida, but they turned 60, and it's the law. —*Jerry Seinfeld*

There is no end to the laws and no beginning to the execution of them. —*Mark Twain*

I was once arrested for walking in someone else's sleep. —*Steven Wright*

I was arrested once for indecent exposure, but they let me off. Lack of evidence. —*Phyllis Diller*

★　★　★　★　★

They say that ignorance of the law is no excuse. I found out when I was in school, the same thing applies to history, geography, and mathematics.

—— ★ ——

There was one guy in our neighborhood who jumped out a window and went up. He was so crooked, he even broke the law of gravity.

—— ★ ——

A guy who lived in our neighborhood used to say that laws were made to be broken. He found out years later that the electric chair was made to be sat in.

——— ★ ———

I have a birthmark on my chest in the shape of a star. When I was a kid and played cowboys, I always had to play the lawman.

My brother always played the cattle rustler. He had a birthmark around his neck in the shape of a rope burn.

——— ★ ———

In the old days, if you broke the law you'd go to jail. Now you go on the Donahue show.

. . . If you break the law and lose weight at the same time, you could make Oprah.

——— ★ ———

They say that Justice is blind, but you wonder, when you read about some cases, if she shouldn't develop a better sense of smell.

——— ★ ———

I got in trouble once and I explained it to my father by saying, "Laws were made to be broken." He said to me as he was taking off his belt, "Guess what behinds were made for."

——— ★ ———

I didn't actually study law in college, but I often had it explained to me by several campus policemen.

——— ★ ———

An officer said to me once, "Do you know it's against the law to drive without a license?" I said, "Then arrest the traffic judge. He's the one who took it away from me."

——— ★ ———

I have a friend who's a law officer and a part-time comedian. It's not working out. Every time he goes onstage he tells the audience that they have the right to remain silent.

. . . And they do.

——— ★ ———

**LAWYERS**

What I need is a lawyer with enough juice to get Ray Charles a driver's license. —*Lenny Bruce*

A lawyer is a man who prevents somebody else from getting your money. —*Milton Berle*

Marriage is really tough because you have to deal with feelings . . . and lawyers. —*Richard Pryor*

I broke a mirror in my house, which is supposed to be 7 years' bad luck. My lawyer thinks he can get me 5.
—*Steven Wright*

My wife and I were considering a divorce, but after pricing lawyers we decided to buy a new car instead.
—*Henny Youngman*

My attorney is brilliant. He didn't bother to graduate from law school; he settled out of class. —*Milton Berle*

A convict sentenced to the electric chair called to ask his attorney's advice. The lawyer said, "Don't sit down."
—*Henny Youngman*

★  ★  ★  ★  ★

I called my lawyer just to say, "Hi, how are you doing?" He said, "Thanks to this call, I'm now $150 richer."

—— ★ ——

The definition of a good lawyer is one who says to you, "You don't need a good lawyer."

—— ★ ——

I not only flunked out of law school; I was also cited for contempt of class.

—— ★ ——

My lawyer got me off on a phony insanity plea. Then when I saw his bill I went insane.

—— ★ ——

My lawyer got me off on a phony insanity plea. Then when I saw his bill I said, "I'd have to be crazy to pay this."

—— ★ ——

When I consulted with my lawyer I said, "I don't have any witnesses, I don't have an alibi, and I don't have any money." He said, "You also don't have an attorney."

—— ★ ——

Lawyers seem to have a way of making mountains out of molehills . . . because you can charge more for a mountain.

—— ★ ——

I think I have to get a higher-priced lawyer. The judge said I was exonerated and my lawyer appealed.

—— ★ ——

My lawyer is very fair-minded. Innocent or guilty, he charges the same fee.

—— ★ ——

I went to see an attorney and said, "I need an attorney to represent me—competently and fairly." He said, "Make up your mind."

—— ★ ——

This man was a very eloquent trial attorney. He graduated from law school magna cum loudmouth.

—— ★ ——

What's rarer than a doctor who can't stand the sight of blood? A lawyer who can't stand the sight of money.

—— ★ ——

I got a jaywalking ticket. Which is the dumbest ticket of all.
I said, "Is this going to go on my record or can I go to
walking school and have this taken off?"

—*Garry Shandling*

I went to court for a parking ticket. I pleaded insanity.
—*Steven Wright*

You know it's time to go on a diet when you're standing
next to your car and get a ticket for double parking.
—*Totie Fields*

In my glove compartment, I had 10 moving-violation ci-
tations, which are like savings bonds—the longer you keep
them, the more they mature. —*Bill Cosby*

★　★　★　★　★

I've never been a very good driver. I got 4 traffic tickets on
my written test.

. . . And two more during the eye exam.

—— ★ ——

I get so many tickets so fast, I had to replace my glove
compartment with a filing cabinet.

—— ★ ——

I've got a master's degree from traffic school.

—— ★ ——

This one town was a real speed trap. I once got a ticket for speeding while I was fixing a flat.

Another policeman there gave me a ticket for having my windshield wipers going the wrong way on a one-way street.

—— ★ ——

A cop gave me a ticket for going the wrong way on a one-way street. I said, "You know, you'd make a lot more money if you let me go and ticket everybody else."

—— ★ ——

A policeman stopped me and said, "Let me see your driver's license." I said, "Officer, you've seen how I drive. Do you think anybody would give me a license?"

—— ★ ——

A policeman stopped me and said, "You know, this car has been reported stolen." I said, "Well, I've found it. Is there a reward?"

—— ★ ——

A cop gave me tickets for speeding, reckless driving, going through a traffic signal, and driving without a license. About the only thing I did right was that I was sitting on the correct side of the vehicle.

—— ★ ——

I'm such an optimist. Every time a policeman drives alongside and asks me to pull over, I think he wants to ask for directions.

—— ★ ——

A police car trailed me for 10 miles and finally pulled me over for speeding. He said, "OK, where's the fire?" I said, "I don't know, officer, but you and I are going to be the first ones there."

—— ★ ——

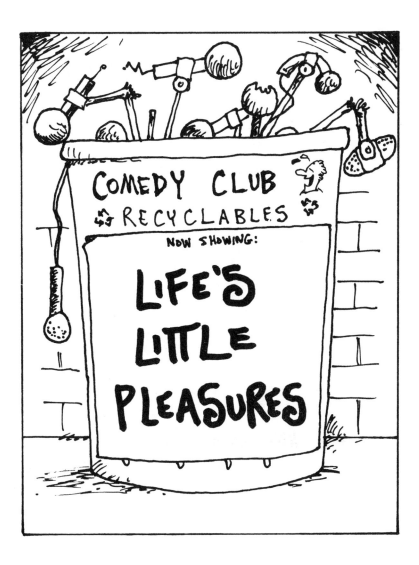

All the things I really like to do are either
immoral, illegal, or fattening.
—*Alexander Woollcott*

## FAVORITE THINGS

The best things in life are free, and the cheesiest things in life are free with a paid subscription to *Sports Illustrated.*
—*Johnny Carson*

Many girls like the quiet things in life, like the folding of a hundred-dollar bill. —*Henny Youngman*

★　★　★　★　★

It's easy to catalogue my favorite things—anything my spouse and the IRS hasn't found out about.

—— ★ ——

One of my favorite things is to have a series of pleasant dreams . . . while I'm at the opera.

—— ★ ——

They say the best things in life are free, but the IRS agent who conducted my audit didn't agree.

—— ★ ——

Life's greatest pleasures are the simple ones, like seeing the driver who cut ahead of you on the freeway pulled over by the police 3 miles down the road.

—— ★ ——

I have a friend who's such a grouch he only has a few favorite things, and he doesn't even like *them.*

—— ★ ——

I have a friend who's a total pessimist. He says life is full of simple little pleasures, but the pain is serious.

—— ★ ——

I enjoy the simple little pleasures of life, but every once in a while, I want a big expensive one thrown in there, too.

—— ★ ——

I have three favorite things: my memories . . . and I forget the other two. —— ★ ——

Oh, sure, I'd like to have all the money in the world, but could I afford to pay the taxes on it?

One bad thing about having all the money in the world—who would you borrow from?

—— ★ ——

All I need to enjoy life are the three "L's": love, laughter, and to hit the lottery.

—— ★ ——

I know the perfect gift for the man who has everything—a burglar alarm. —*Milton Berle*

You know what I got for Father's Day? The bills from Mother's Day. —*Henny Youngman*

I gave my wife a gift certificate for Christmas. She ran out to exchange it for a bigger size. —*Milton Berle*

★ ★ ★ ★ ★

My wife said, "That gift you bought me for my 35th birthday was perfect." I said, "It should be. This is the fifth year in a row I've bought something for your 35th birthday."

—— ★ ——

I asked my wife what she wanted for our anniversary. She told me to buy something for the house. So I bought a round of drinks.

—— ★ ——

My spouse said, "I really don't want a gift this year. Let's just do something together." So we had a fight about my not buying a gift.

—— ★ ——

My husband bought me the perfect gift for my birthday. It's something he's always wanted.

—— ★ ——

I think the best thing about receiving the perfect gift is taking it back and exchanging it for something better.

—— ★ ——

My wife said she bought me the perfect gift the other day. She'll give it to me when I'm worthy of it.

—— ★ ——

It's not the gift that counts; it's the thought behind it. That's kind of what I told my spouse on our last anniversary: "I *thought* I got you something."

—— ★ ——

They say it's better to give than receive. I've discovered with some gifts, that's true.

—— ★ ——

For our anniversary I presented my wife with an all-expense-paid trip for two to Tahiti. She's been busy ever since trying to decide who to take with her.

—— ★ ——

I told my wife for my birthday I wanted her to give me something I'd never forget. She gave me a string to tie around my finger.

—— ★ ——

I like to receive the gift of money. You can exchange it for so many nice things.

—— ★ ——

I told my wife I wanted an antique as a gift. She had my birth certificate framed.

— ★ —

I have a car that I call Flattery because it gets me nowhere.
—*Henny Youngman*

I've been complimented many times, and that always embarrasses me. I always feel they have not said enough.
—*Mark Twain*

I can live for two months on a good compliment.
—*Mark Twain*

He paid me a compliment. He said I looked like a breath of spring. Well, he didn't use those words. He said I looked like the end of a hard winter. —*Minnie Pearl*

People tell me, "Gee, you look good." There are three ages of man: youth, middle age, and "gee, you look good."
—*Red Skelton*

I got a wonderful tribute at the airport. They fired 21 shots in the air in my honor. Of course, it would've been nicer if they'd waited for the plane to land. —*Bob Hope*

★　★　★　★　★

This man's an incurable liar, except when he's complimenting me.

— ★ —

I've received 10 compliments today. Two of them from other people.

———— ★ ————

Have you noticed? Celebrities all hate critics, but quote them when they give good reviews.

———— ★ ————

I graciously accept all compliments. One can't argue with the truth.

———— ★ ————

I told my mother-in-law that in 25 years of being married to her daughter, she's never said anything nice about me. She asked for a little more time.

———— ★ ————

If you compliment me, I'll compliment you. There's a good chance one of us might be telling the truth.

———— ★ ————

Remember, you can catch more flies with a teaspoon of honey than with a barrel of vinegar. Of course, what you're going to do with a bunch of sticky flies is your problem.

———— ★ ————

I love to listen to compliments. I feel humility should be saved for those who have truly earned it.

———— ★ ————

Some people say "thank you" after receiving a compliment. I simply nod in agreement.

———— ★ ————

As far as I'm concerned, you can keep all your compliments to yourself. I much prefer a cash reward.

———— ★ ————

My spouse always finds some little thing in the morning to compliment me about. Oh, sometimes it takes an hour or more. . . .

———— ★ ————

I've been collecting compliments all my life. So far I've gotten three.

———— ★ ————

When the insects take over the world, we hope they will remember with gratitude how we took them along on all our picnics. —*Bill Vaughan*

Watermelon—it's a good fruit. You eat, you drink, you wash your face. —*Enrico Caruso*

The best form of exercise is picnics. You can use up 2,000 calories trying to keep the ants and flies away from the potato salad. —*Jack E. Leonard*

Insects must have brains. How else would they know that you're going on a picnic? —*Milton Berle*

★ ★ ★ ★ ★

Picnics were invented to justify all that potato salad.

—— ★ ——

The problem with picnics is that they're always held on a holiday—when the ants have the day off, too.

—— ★ ——

Picnics are fun. Anytime there are that many men walking around in short pants, it's got to be a lot of laughs.

—— ★ ——

You know the rarest thing in the world? An ant who over-sleeps on the Fourth of July.

—— ★ ——

So many ants showed up at our picnic that they won the tug-of-war. —— ★ ——

I think history will prove that picnics were invented either by a colony of hungry ants or by a mayonnaise salesman.

———— ★ ————

Picnics are always held outdoors because that's where you want to be when the hard-boiled eggs go bad.

———— ★ ————

Our family is so large that every year I go to the cousins' picnic to meet new friends.

———— ★ ————

Talk about strange bedfellows. How about all the ants who show up at the exterminators' picnic.

———— ★ ————

Our family always asks Aunt Matilda to make her tuna surprise for the cousins' picnic. It's the best thing we've found yet to keep the flies away.

. . . Or to punish those flies who do show up.

———— ★ ————

The bad news is that I got poison ivy at our cousins' picnic. The worse news is that I got it from Aunt Matilda's green salad.

———— ★ ————

We always end our cousins' picnic with a fireworks display—Aunt Matilda and Uncle Harvey's marital problems.

———— ★ ————

THE BEACH

When I go to the beach I don't tan, I stroke.
—*Woody Allen*

The girls are wearing less and less on the beach, which is perfect for me because my memory is starting to go.
—*Bob Hope*

This girl was so thin every time she went to the beach, a dog buried her.　　　　　　　　　　　　—*Milton Berle*

The town was so dull that when the tide went out it refused to come back.　　　　　　　　　　—*Fred Allen*

I never expected to see the day when girls would get sunburned in the places they do today.　　　—*Will Rogers*

I went to the beach the other day. I held my stomach in so much I threw out my back.　　　　　　—*Milton Berle*

I won't say her bathing suit was skimpy, but I've seen more cotton in the top of an aspirin bottle.　—*Henny Youngman*

★　　★　　★　　★　　★

I don't look good on the beach. I look like I'm wearing my inner tube internally.

—— ★ ——

The beach is where you wear practically nothing at all and it fills with sand.

—— ★ ——

Bathing suits don't shrink in water. They shrink when they're stored in the closet during the winter.

—— ★ ——

Vacation is when you can lie on the beach and get burned by the sun and also by the hotel where you're booked.

—— ★ ——

The sales clerk said, "That bathing suit fits you perfectly." I said, "Sure, that's what you said about the one I bought here last year, too."

—— ★ ——

I bought a bathing suit that said, "one size fits all" and proved it wrong.

—— ★ ——

I look so bad in a bathing suit, the lifeguard asked me to go for a swim the other day—to scare any sharks away.

—— ★ ——

I had a close call at the beach last week. I swallowed too much sand from trying to suck in my stomach.

—— ★ ——

The other day I sat for hours on the beach hoping to watch the sunrise. Finally someone was nice enough to tell me I was facing the wrong way.

. . . I got a terrible burn on my back.

—— ★ ——

Last week I fell asleep on the beach with my mouth open. My tongue got sunburned.

. . . It took a good two weeks before I could say "Theophilus."

—— ★ ——

All you need to be a fisherman is patience and a worm.
—*Herb Shriner*

You never see a fish on the wall with its mouth shut.
—*Sally Berger*

Good fishing is just a matter of timing. You have to get there yesterday.
—*Milton Berle*

My husband is one of those fishermen who wear those boots that extend up to the armpits, so that when the water pours in, you are assured of drowning instantly.

—*Erma Bombeck*

★　★　★　★　★

If you don't do anything the entire day, you're called a bum. If you do it in a boat, you're called a fisherman.

I once knew a one-armed fisherman. He had a terrible time telling you how big the one that got away was.

Every time I try fishing, the fish aren't biting but the mosquitoes are.

I think someday I'll go out in a boat and try to go "mosquitoing."

I went trout fishing one day with my dumb cousin. As we stood waist-deep in the water he said, "You know, I wish I was a lot taller because someday I'd like to go deep-sea fishing."

They say you have to be smart to be a good fisherman. I say all you need is a hook and a dumb fish.

I knew an old fellow who told me once, "In order to catch fish, you have to think like a fish." He's gone now. He drowned one night in his sleep.

Fishing is great recreation. It's just about the most fun you can have with a worm on a string.

I used to enjoy fishing tremendously until one day I happened to look at it from the worm's point of view.

The game warden said, "You've got a worm on your line, you got the line in the water, and you tell me you're not fishing. What exactly are you doing?" The man said, "I'm carrying out a punishment. This particular worm has been accused of witchcraft."

—— ★ ——

I went fishing once, but never again—not until someone invents self-cleaning fish.

—— ★ ——

To listen to fishermen, you wonder why small fish never get away.

—— ★ ——

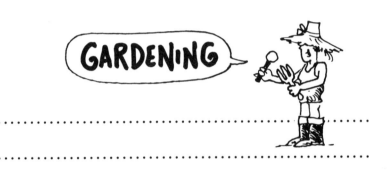

.................................................

.................................................

Did you see the pictures of the moon? They must have the same gardener I have.    *—Harry Hershfield*

I like to tease my plants. I water them with ice cubes.    *—Steven Wright*

I don't exactly have a green thumb. I once killed a flagpole.    *—Milton Berle*

I don't have the knack for growing house plants. I bought a hanging fern and the rope died.    *—Milton Berle*

I have bad luck with plants. I bought a philodendron and put it in the kitchen. It drank my soup.    *—Joan Rivers*

★    ★    ★    ★    ★

I have bad luck with plants. I have a chia pet that attacked the mailman.

— ★ —

I'm a terrible gardener. I tried to plant some flowers along my driveway. The asphalt died.

— ★ —

I'm a bad gardener. I have a green thumb that has dry rot.

— ★ —

I bought some artificial roses for my house. They were eaten by artificial aphids.

— ★ —

I can't do anything right with plants. I bought a Venus fly trap. It turned out to be a vegetarian.

When I got it home, it attacked the zipper on my pants.

— ★ —

I have a clinging vine that I call butterfingers.

— ★ —

I can't raise house plants at all. The guy at the nursery said I should talk to them. All I can say to them is, "Rest in peace."

— ★ —

Other people own gardening tools; I have lethal weapons.

— ★ —

I'm such a terrible gardener they have a wanted poster of me hanging at the local nursery.

— ★ —

I paid a fortune for a philodendron. It died before I learned how to spell it.

— ★ —

I'm such a terrible gardener, if anyone comes to my yard and asks, "What kind of plant is that?" I say, "A dead one."

— ★ —

WALKING

Everywhere is within walking distance if you have the time.
—*Steven Wright*

I like long walks, especially when they are taken by people who annoy me. —*Fred Allen*

My grandmother started walking 5 miles a day when she was 60. She's 93 today and we don't know where the hell she is. —*Ellen Degeneres*

Most people agree that walks are good for your health. Where I live in Beverly Hills, nobody walks. I've got one neighbor who has a little car to drive to his big car.
—*George Burns*

The true charm of pedestrianism does not lie in the walking, or in the scenery, but in the talking. —*Mark Twain*

★ ★ ★ ★ ★

I own a pair of microwave walking shoes. I can now take a leisurely walk in the country in 2½ minutes.

—— ★ ——

The only thing better than an early-morning walk with someone you love is to have someone you love take an early-morning walk without you and then wake you when she gets home. —— ★ ——

Walking is probably the greatest form of exercise there is, unless you're in water. Then swimming is better.

—— ★ ——

Walking can be a relaxing pastime or a beneficial exercise. For me, it's just a way to get back and forth to the car.

—— ★ ——

My advice to people who jog is to leave earlier and walk.

—— ★ ——

I looked at a good pair of walking shoes the other day. They cost $120. For that kind of money I could take a cab.

Imagine that . . . $120 for a pair of walking shoes. Centipedes don't realize how lucky they are that they can go barefoot.

—— ★ ——

Short walks can be very romantic—especially if they're up the center aisle of a church.

—— ★ ——

Sometimes I dream I'm walking, which is nice. I get my rest and exercise all at the same time.

It's a fair exchange—I usually dream when I'm walking, too.

—— ★ ——

Last night I ordered an entire meal in French and even the waiter was surprised. I was in a Chinese restaurant.
—*Henny Youngman*

My split personality is getting worse. Yesterday I ate in a restaurant alone and asked for two checks.
—*Rodney Dangerfield*

I once crossed a waiter with a tiger. I don't know what I got but I tip him big.                              —*Milton Berle*

Fang took me to a restaurant that he said was secluded. That means the Board of Health can't find it.
                                                —*Phyllis Diller*

I was arrested today for scalping low numbers at the deli.
                                                —*Steven Wright*

A holdup man walks into a Chinese restaurant, and he says, "Give me all your money." The man says, "To go?"
                                                —*Slappy White*

I've been trying to get my husband to take me out to dinner for so long, that when he finally said yes, I couldn't eat.
                                                —*Phyllis Diller*

I was in a restaurant. I called the waitress over and said, "This coffee isn't fit for a pig." She said, "Oh, I'll take it away and bring you some that is."          —*Milton Berle*

★　　★　　★　　★　　★

My wife says the nicest thing about eating out is that no matter what you order someone else is going to have to do the dishes.

—— ★ ——

When we were getting ready to go out and eat, my wife said, "I feel like a hamburger tonight." And she must have, because she put on secret sauce instead of lipstick.

—— ★ ——

My wife said, "Get your elbows off the table." So, I did and my face fell in the soup.

—— ★ ——

We went to a very expensive restaurant the other night. When you come in, they let you keep your hat and coat, but you have to check your wallet.

—— ★ ——

This restaurant charged exorbitant prices. I asked the waiter, "What's the catch of the day?" He said, "You are."

—— ★ ——

The portions at this restaurant were so small I had to fill up on parsley.

—— ★ ——

This restaurant had little asterisks next to those menu items that were supposed to be good for your heart. I noticed there were no asterisks next to any of the prices.

—— ★ ——

When we left this expensive restaurant the maître d' said, "Come back again." I said, "Why? To visit my money?"

—— ★ ——

What a dump this restaurant was. Fly swatters were an item on the menu.

—— ★ ——

This restaurant was so cheap and so lousy, they gave us the check faceup and turned the food over.

—— ★ ——

Never eat at a restaurant that lists Pepto-Bismol soufflé as a dessert.

—— ★ ——

This restaurant was so bad I asked the waiter, "What do you recommend?" He said, "Get out while you still can."

—— ★ ——

I went to one restaurant and ordered Tuna-Fish Surprise. The surprise was that the tuna fish was tainted.

—— ★ ——

The waiter at one restaurant advised me that they were no longer offering the special of the day. It exploded.

—— ★ ——

Never eat at a restaurant where the place mats have instructions for the Heimlich maneuver printed on them.

—— ★ ——

Never eat at a restaurant where menu items are marked with an asterisk, signifying those items covered by the restaurant's insurance policy.

I asked the waiter what was in the veal Caribbean. He said, "I don't know, and considering the condition of the chef, he probably doesn't know either."

The food at this restaurant was so bad that in the kitchen the flies threw themselves at the fly paper.

. . . It was safer than landing on the special of the day.

I said to my waiter, "What would you recommend?" He said, "The restaurant down the street."

This restaurant was so bad that I not only had a fly in my soup, but the entire pair of trousers.

This restaurant was so bad that their doggie bags were marked "not for consumption by real dogs."

The food here was bad. I said to the waiter, "There's a fly in my soup." He said, "Let's hope for his sake he doesn't swallow any."

I went to a Middle Eastern restaurant where I knew they served camel meat. I asked the waiter for a glass of water, and they didn't bring it for 10 days.

. . . I ordered a hamburger and the waiter asked, "One hump or two?"

This restaurant knew their food was bad. As we left, the maître d' said, "Please come back and see us when you've recovered."

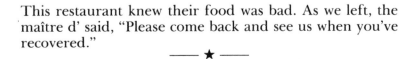

There are only a few things in this life that give me pleasure, and I can't stand them.
—*Gene Perret*

TAXES

The income tax people are very nice. They're letting me keep my own mother.
—*Henny Youngman*

It's getting to the point where you need more brains to make out the income-tax forms than to make the income.
—*Henny Youngman*

If you owe the government $5,000, you make out your return for $10,000. The government owes you $5,000, and you owe them $5,000. So you're even. —*Gracie Allen*

Income tax is the fairest tax of all. It gives everyone an equal chance at poverty.
—*Bob Hope*

Any reasonable taxation should be based on the slogan "Soak the rich."
—*Heywood Broun*

It's true that nothing is certain but death and taxes. Sometimes I wish they came in that order.
—*Sam Levenson*

What is the difference between a taxidermist and a tax collector? The taxidermist takes only your skin.
—*Mark Twain*

April 15 . . . the day when millions of Americans realize they've got an extra person on their payroll—Uncle Sam.
—*Henny Youngman*

The IRS has streamlined its tax form for this year. It goes like this: (A) How much did you make last year? (B) How much have you left? (C) Send B.
—*Henny Youngman*

★   ★   ★   ★   ★

Taxes are our annual reminder that the land of the free *ain't*.

Tax time is when the piper must be paid. Most people don't object to that. It's when the piper asks for an audit that they get scared.

They say that only two things are certain in this life—death and taxes. The difference is that after death you don't care whether you get audited or not.

I fill out the short tax form every year. I send a postcard to the IRS that says, "What do I owe you?"

We need taxes. Good government costs money, and so does ours.

When they said we had a government of the people, by the people, and for the people, I didn't know they were talking about who was going to pick up the tab.

Someone once said, "Taxation without representation is tyranny." With representation, it's no bed of roses, either.

It's pretty much common knowledge that you can't take it with you. The IRS is here just to make doubly sure of that.

The next time you send in your taxes to pay for our government, think about this: If you saw our government in a store for that price, would you buy it?

The income-tax instruction booklet gets more and more complicated each year. They should pay *us* to read that thing.

Now they want to print tax instruction in Spanish, Chinese, Japanese. I don't care what language they put it in, it's all Greek to me. ——— ★ ———

I always go out and have a couple of drinks before filling out my tax returns. I'm never sure I'll be able to afford them afterwards. ——— ★ ———

I took a physical for some life insurance. All they would give me was fire and theft. —*Henny Youngman*

I don't want to tell you how much insurance I carry, but all I can say is: When I go, *they* go. —*Jack Benny*

There are worse things in life than death. Have you ever spent an evening with an insurance salesman?
—*Woody Allen*

And what is this life insurance? You're betting that you die. If you live, you lose. —*Alan King*

I just got my TV set insured. If it breaks down, they send me a pair of binoculars so I can watch my neighbor's set.
—*Henny Youngman*

I'm paying so much in insurance to take care of the future that I'm starving to death in the present. —*Alan King*

A man had no life insurance, but he did have fire insurance. So his wife had him cremated. —*Milton Berle*

★　★　★　★　★

I don't have life insurance, only fire and theft. So my wife is hoping that when I'm on my sickbed, someone steals me.

—— ★ ——

I have extensive earthquake and fire insurance on my home. I call it my Shake 'n Bake insurance.

—— ★ ——

I just took a physical for my life insurance policy, and the doctor said I should live forever. It's the only way I'll break even.

—— ★ ——

I have fire, theft, collision, and personal liability insurance on my car. The other day it ran away from home.

—— ★ ——

My insurance salesman doesn't bother me anymore since I took out a $100,000 life insurance policy. I took it out on him.

—— ★ ——

Insurance policies always exclude "acts of God." What do they think dying is—a recreational pastime?

—— ★ ——

My insurance agent recommended a double-indemnity policy. I get double for accidental death. Does he really think I would die on purpose?

—— ★ ——

I don't like insurance companies. I get the money when I die, but they get to use those beautiful office buildings while I'm still alive.

—— ★ ——

I've got so much life insurance I have to die. I need the money to keep up the payments.

—— ★ ——

I don't have life insurance because I'm as healthy as a horse. When I go, someone can sell my carcass to the glue factory.

—— ★ ——

I can always worry about life insurance tomorrow. When I hit a day when I don't have a tomorrow, that's the day I'll buy the insurance.

—— ★ ——

My agent says life insurance is an investment in the future. I said, "That's strange. I don't collect until I don't have a future."

—— ★ ——

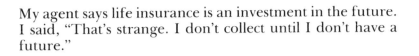

What did the bald man say when he got a comb for his birthday? "Thanks very much. I'll never part with it."
*—Larry Wilde*

He really isn't bald-headed—he just has a tall face.
*—Milton Berle*

The best thing about being bald is when her folks come home, all you have to do is straighten your tie.
*—Milton Berle*

★　★　★　★　★

My Uncle Phil says he's not bald. He's just taller than his hair.

—— ★ ——

My Uncle Ralph always thought he had wavy hair until he went bald. It was his head that was wavy.

—— ★ ——

My doctor said he would cure my baldness but it would cost me $3,000. I said, "What do I get if it doesn't work?" He said, "A free comb."

—— ★ ——

My Uncle Phil is totally bald. My Aunt Myrtle calls him the human thumb.

—— ★ ——

My Uncle Phil tried to invent a lotion that would grow hair on a billiard ball. It worked—partly. He's still bald, but he likes to sleep at night on the pool table.

—— ★ ——

My Uncle Ralph sprained his neck trying to cure his baldness. He grew a beard and tried to put his head on upside down.

—— ★ ——

My Uncle Phil is so bald that at night Aunt Myrtle uses his head to read by.

—— ★ ——

I'm not really bald. My hair is just hibernating.

—— ★ ——

My uncle says he has a "receding hairline." It has receded all the way back to his neck.

—— ★ ——

The bad news is some bald people still have dandruff. The good news is they have a lot more room for it.

—— ★ ——

I asked my doctor, "What's the best thing for baldness?" He said, "A sense of humor."

—— ★ ——

ARITHMETIC

A teacher asked, "If you had 5 apples and I asked for 1, how many would you have left?" A boy answered, "Five."
—*Milton Berle*

I was raised in the days of the times tables. We used to recite times tables for company. —*Sam Levenson*

★　★　★　★　★

My dad says I should study my numbers hard. He says arithmetic is something you can always count on.

—— ★ ——

Professor: If you have 5 apples and I take away 4 of them, what will you have left?
Student: One apple—to throw at you for taking my other 4.

—— ★ ——

I have a friend who is so bad at arithmetic he has to take off his shoes and socks to count how many fingers he has.

—— ★ ——

Professor: If you have 26 cents in one pants pocket and 32 cents in the other, how much money do you have?
Student: None. All my pants have holes in the pockets.

—— ★ ——

Professor: What are prime numbers?
Billy: Numbers that are on television between 8 o'clock and 11 o'clock.

—— ★ ——

Professor:   What do you get if you multiply 13,362 by 476?

Student:   Confused.

—— ★ ——

Teacher:   If you have 12 cents in one pants pocket and 6 cents in the other pants pocket, what do you have?

Billy:   A lot of trouble because my mother gave me a dollar and a quarter when I left for school this morning.

—— ★ ——

I'm very bad at arithmetic. I can count from 1 to 100, but I have trouble putting the numbers in order.

—— ★ ——

Our teacher said, "Three men dig a hole in 9 hours. How long would it take 6 men to dig it?" I said, "Why don't they use the hole the other 3 guys just dug?"

—— ★ ——

I've flunked arithmetic three times now. Once more will make it five.

—— ★ ——

Our teacher said, "What would you get if you divided 7,938 by 143?" I said, "Probably another 'F' in arithmetic."

—— ★ ——

The local groceries are all out of broccoli, loccoli.

—*Roy Blount Jr.*

I said to my son, "Finish up all your meat, and you'll grow up and be just like Daddy." Since then he only eats vegetables.                                    —*Rodney Dangerfield*

A vegetarian is a person who won't eat anything that can have children.                                    —*David Brenner*

★  ★  ★  ★  ★

My mother used to say, "There are places in this world where people are going to bed hungry." I would say, "Do you really think sending them cauliflower would change that?"

——— ★ ———

A vegetarian is someone who doesn't eat meat and looks funny at people who do.

——— ★ ———

Vegetables are of less importance than meat. Do you think people would really care if lima beans got tangled up in the tuna nets?

——— ★ ———

To me, vegetables are not a food; they're a food accessory.

——— ★ ———

If you really wanted people to eat something, would you name it "succotash"?

——— ★ ———

After a minor accident, one driver said, "If I weren't a priest, I'd chew your ear off." The other driver said, "Then we're equal. I'm a vegetarian."

——— ★ ———

I heard one vegetarian say, "Boy, I'm so hungry I could eat a horseradish."

——— ★ ———

Technically, the potato is not a vegetable. It's something you push the vegetables against when you're trying to get them on your fork.

Spoken by the lone vegetarian in a cannibal tribe: "No thanks, I'll just munch on his clothing."

—— ★ ——

There's one thing you very rarely hear said about vegetables: "It tastes a little bit like chicken."

—— ★ ——

My mom had a unique way of trying to get me to eat my vegetables. She'd say, "You eat every single thing on your plate, or you'll be sent to bed without your supper."

. . . And I was so dumb, it worked.

—— ★ ——

If at first you don't succeed, try, try again. Then quit. No use being a damn fool about it.

—*W. C. Fields*

. . . . . . . . . . . . . . . . . . . . . . . . . . . . . . . . . . . . . . . . . . . . .

. . . . . . . . . . . . . . . . . . . . . . . . . . . . . . . . . . . . . . . . . . . . .

They say behind every successful man, there's a woman. Take a good look at me—can you picture what I got behind me? —*Rodney Dangerfield*

There's no secret about success. Did you ever know a successful man who didn't tell you all about it.
—*Kin Hubbard*

I was voted the dropout most likely to succeed.
—*Jan Murray*

My father was a very successful businessman, but he was ruined in the crash. . . . A big stockbroker jumped out of a window and fell on his pushcart. —*Jackie Mason*

That's all there is to success is satisfaction. —*Will Rogers*

If at first you don't succeed . . . cheat. —*Red Buttons*

The man with a new idea is a crank until the idea succeeds.
—*Mark Twain*

All you need in this life is ignorance and confidence, and then success is sure. —*Mark Twain*

We can't all be heroes, because somebody has to sit on the curb and clap as they go by. —*Will Rogers*

★　★　★　★　★

I know you won't let success go to your head. Nothing else has.

— ★ —

You've worked hard for everything you have. You obviously didn't get it on personality.

— ★ —

If at first you don't succeed, try, try again. Failures like you need something to keep them occupied.

— ★ —

There's only one thing keeping me from being a success— abject failure.

— ★ —

The one thing my mother wanted was a successful son. I did my part. I urged her to have more children.

— ★ —

If at first you don't succeed, become a consultant and teach someone else how to do it.

— ★ —

I consider myself a success because I always wanted to be the biggest failure in the world.

— ★ —

Everybody wants to be more successful than the next guy. So try to stand next to some guy who's not doing that well.

— ★ —

I've been a success and I've been a failure. Failure doesn't take as long.

. . . But it's more enduring.

— ★ —

If you want to avoid traffic, get on the road to success.

— ★ —

A friend of mine started a business teaching people how to be successful. He had to. He needed the money.

— ★ —

OPPORTUNITY

I was seldom able to see an opportunity until it had ceased to be one.
—*Mark Twain*

Some people don't recognize opportunity when it knocks because it comes in the form of hard work.
—*H. L. Mencken*

★　★　★　★　★

Opportunity only knocks once, which means it would make a lousy Avon lady.

—— ★ ——

Whenever someone tells you, "This is the opportunity of a lifetime," ask if they're referring to your lifetime or theirs.

—— ★ ——

It's so unfair. Opportunity only knocks once, but my car knocks every time I drive it over 40 miles an hour.

—— ★ ——

My brother-in-law is so lazy, every time there's a knock on the door, he pretends he's not home. He's afraid it might be opportunity.

—— ★ ——

The young worker said, "All I want is an opportunity," but he wasn't being truthful. He wanted a salary, too.

—— ★ ——

He said, "All I want is an opportunity to show you what I can do." He showed us, and now he's looking for an opportunity someplace else.

—— ★ ——

It's a cop-out to say that opportunity only knocks once. There are plenty of seashells in the world, but how many of them knock on your door more than once?

— ★ —

Opportunity knocked at my door once. I must have been in the shower at the time.

— ★ —

Any time someone tells you they're offering you the opportunity of a lifetime, be careful. It'll probably cost your life savings.

— ★ —

Many people go out and become a success while others are sitting home waiting for opportunity to knock.

— ★ —

Opportunity is nature's way of saying, "Hey, if you don't make it, dummy, it's your own fault."

— ★ —

What I can't figure out is how come opportunity knocks once but the postman always rings twice?

— ★ —

Money is better than poverty, if only for financial reasons.
—*Woody Allen*

A man who has $11 million is just as happy as a man who has . . . $12 million. —*Joe E. Lewis*

Two very rich people got divorced and their lawyers lived happily ever after. —*Milton Berle*

These people were so rich they had a Persian rug made out of real Persians. —*Henny Youngman*

★　★　★　★　★

Money can't buy happiness, but then neither can poverty.

. . . Also, with money, you can be miserable in much better surroundings.

—— ★ ——

It's true that money can't buy happiness, but poverty can't even buy groceries.

—— ★ ——

I've always wanted to be filthy rich. So far, I've only gotten the first part.

—— ★ ——

Someday my ship will come in. With my luck, when it does, it'll probably break down my dock.

—— ★ ——

I have a friend who has plenty of money, but is he happy? I don't know because since he got rich he doesn't hang around with me.

—— ★ ——

I'm pretty close to being a millionaire. I'm only 7 figures away.

It's been said, "If you cast your bread upon the water it will come back to you a hundredfold." That's pretty good advice if you like to eat soggy sandwiches.

—— ★ ——

A poor person can have a maid, a butler, and a chauffeur, too. That's if he can find three people dumb enough to work for a percentage.

—— ★ ——

The rich get richer and the poor get poorer. Me? I've got just enough to get bad credit ratings.

—— ★ ——

Someday I'd like to be rich enough to get out of all the trouble my poverty got me into.

—— ★ ——

I call my weekly salary my take-home pay because it's the only place I can afford to go with it.

—— ★ ——

Nothing is all wrong. Even a clock that stops is right twice a day.
—*Morey Amsterdam*

This guy is such a loser he gives failure a bad name.
—*Joey Adams*

If at first you don't succeed, failure may be your thing.
—*Milton Berle*

★  ★  ★  ★  ★

I am not a failure; I'm a success that hasn't happened yet.

My credit card company says they're not cancelling my card; they're just holding it until I happen.

—— ★ ——

Some endeavors are doomed to failure, like trying to jump across a well in two jumps.

—— ★ ——

My uncle has a bright philosophy. He says, "I am not a failure. I'm a success who has no money and can't get a job."

—— ★ ——

I picked up a self-help book that said on the cover, "There is no such thing as failure." Then two clerks chased me out of the store because of my failure to pay for the book.

—— ★ ——

A wise soldier once said that retreat is just fighting in the opposite direction. By the same token, I feel I'm not a failure; I'm just very successful at not getting what I want.

—— ★ ——

Some say that failure is a state of mind. I'm in the state of mind that I haven't paid any of my bills in over 4 months.

—— ★ ——

My dad always taught me: "There's no such thing as failure." Then one day he asked to see my report card. I told him, "There's no such thing as my report card."

—— ★ ——

Some sage once advised that every failure leads to an eventual success. He was right. I failed to stay on my diet, and now I successfully can't fit into any of my clothes.

—— ★ ——

The blowhard's success formula: If at first you don't succeed, lie, lie again.

—— ★ ——

Failure is nothing to be ashamed of. Just look upon it as success that happened for somebody else.

—— ★ ——

If at first you don't succeed, pretend that's not what you were trying to do in the first place.

—— ★ ——

Anyone who believes there is no such thing as failure has never tried to play golf.

—— ★ ——

**Nothing is more irritating than not being invited to a party you wouldn't be caught dead at.**

*—Bill Vaughan*

My wife wanted a foreign convertible for her birthday. I got her a rickshaw. *—Henny Youngman*

I never know what to get my father for his birthday. I gave him $100 and said, "Buy yourself something that will make your life easier." So he went out and bought a present for my mother. *—Rita Rudner*

Marriage is the alliance of two people, one of whom never remembers birthdays and the other who never forgets them. *—Ogden Nash*

You know you're old when everybody goes to your birthday party and stands around the cake just to get warm. *—George Burns*

I walked into a store and said, "This is my wife's birthday. I'd like to buy her a beautiful fountain pen." The clerk said, "A little surprise, huh?" I said, "Yeah. She's expecting a Cadillac." *—Henny Youngman*

★ ★ ★ ★ ★

Marlene: Last night I threw myself a surprise birthday party.

Sarah: If you threw it yourself, what was the surprise?

Marlene: That my birthday is not until next February.

—— ★ ——

I'm such a famous person that my birthday has been declared a national holiday. If you don't believe me, just ask George Washington. He was born on the same day.

—— ★ ——

My grandfather's birthday party was postponed on account of rain. It was indoors. But he's so old, all the candles on his cake set off the sprinkler system.

—— ★ ——

Remember, you're as young as you feel. If you don't feel anything, you're old.

—— ★ ——

I suppose I'm getting up in years. If I were a bottle of wine I'd be worth a fortune now.

—— ★ ——

You know you're getting old when one year between birthdays is not enough time to blow out all the candles on your cake.

—— ★ ——

What ought to be done to the man who invented the celebration of anniversaries? Mere killing would be too light.
—*Mark Twain*

My wife said for our anniversary she wanted to go someplace she'd never been before. I said, "How 'bout the kitchen."
—*Rodney Dangerfield*

★    ★    ★    ★    ★

On our anniversary, my wife told me, "I know I married you for better, for worse, for richer, for poorer, but I've changed my mind. I'm ready now for better and richer."

—— ★ ——

My wife and I got divorced on our anniversary. That's a pretty nice anniversary gift—half of everything I own.

My wife and I have been married for 12 years with time off for good behavior.

Our kids threw a surprise 25th anniversary party for us. It was a real surprise since we were divorced 4 years ago.

On our anniversary, I told my wife I was very proud to be married to the same woman for 25 years. She said, "After 25 years of being married to you, I'm not quite the same woman."

The 1st anniversary is paper. So on that day, my wife had me served.

On our anniversary my wife and I went back to the hotel where we had our honeymoon 25 years before. It was run-down, too.

I told my bride she gets more beautiful with each passing year. As an anniversary gift, she gave me a pair of glasses.

My mother told me on her 60th wedding anniversary that marriage gets easier as you get older. She said, "There are many things I can't stand about your father, but I'll be damned if I can remember what they are."

One year I forgot our anniversary. For the rest of the year my wife forgot my name.

. . . And to set a place for me at dinner.

GRADUATION

A crazy guy ran up to me today and kept yelling, "Call me a doctor. Call me a doctor." I said, "What's the matter? Are you sick?" He said, "No, I just graduated from medical school."
—*Henny Youngman*

★   ★   ★   ★   ★

My mom and dad were so proud of me when I graduated from high school—so were my wife and kids.

—— ★ ——

My dad gave me the best advice as they handed me my high school diploma. He yelled, "Take it and run, son."

—— ★ ——

I hated to graduate from high school. It was ten of the happiest years of my life.

—— ★ ——

When I graduated from college I had no idea what I was going to do, but I had a piece of paper that said I knew how to do it.

—— ★ ——

A college diploma is a piece of paper that says your education is now complete; now it's time to get off your butt and start paying for it.

—— ★ ——

A young friend of mine wrote: "Dear Mom and Dad, Since I graduated from law school today, I will no longer have to write and ask you for money. Now I know how to demand it."

—— ★ ——

Another youngster wrote: "Dear Mom and Dad, I graduated from medical school, so you no longer have to send me money. Just have your insurance company send it."

—— ★ ——

I couldn't believe it when I graduated with honors. Neither could the school. That's why they made me retake all the tests.

—— ★ ——

I hate parties. I'm always answering questions like, "You said you were a friend of *whose*?"     —*Rodney Dangerfield*

I remember one party was called off because I *was* in town.
—*Rodney Dangerfield*

A cocktail party is a gathering where sandwiches and friends are cut into little pieces.     —*Milton Berle*

I once went to a masquerade party wearing boxer shorts. I have terrible varicose veins so I went as a road map.
—*Woody Allen*

★   ★   ★   ★   ★

It was a great cocktail party. We killed three pitchers of martinis and seven reputations.

—— ★ ——

Good advice for cocktail parties: If you can't say something nice about someone, just hold your drink and listen to those who can't, either.

—— ★ ——

Many cocktail parties are a group of people having a lousy time trying to have a good time.

—— ★ ——

A stranger came up to me at a cocktail party and said, "Who do you know at this party?" I said, "Absolutely no one, and I'm trying to keep it that way."

—— ★ ——

I think I had too much to drink at the party. When I put my foot in my mouth, it came out pickled.

—— ★ ——

I asked my wife if I got too loud and obnoxious at the party. She said, "Let's put it this way—it was the kind of party where a good time was had by one."

—— ★ ——

I went to one cocktail party that was really a masquerade party. Everyone was disguised as someone who wanted to be there.

—— ★ ——

One of the worst feelings in the world is to show up at a costume party not wearing a costume—and no one notices.

—— ★ ——

A bald head comes in handy for costume parties. I just polish it and go as a lighthouse.

—— ★ ——

A gentleman came to a costume party absolutely naked. He said, "I'm dressed as Adam." The host said, "Where's Eve?" He said, "I was hoping to meet her here."

—— ★ ——

I went to one costume party dressed as Joan of Arc. They set my place for dinner *on* the barbecue.

—— ★ ——

Twenty-two of my friends and I went to a costume party dressed as circus clowns. That way we could all go in one car.

—— ★ ——

Gene:   Did you read my last book?
Reader:   Oh, I hope so.

—*Gene Perret*

**BOOMERANGS**

An economist is a guy who'd throw you a boomerang for your birthday.
—*Milton Berle*

★   ★   ★   ★   ★

The boomerang is a stick that will always come back to you when you throw it. It's for kids who like to play "fetch," but don't own a dog.

—— ★ ——

The man who invented the boomerang was hurt in an accident. Right after he invented it, he forgot to duck.

—— ★ ——

The question is: If a boomerang always comes back to you after you throw it, why throw it in the first place?

—— ★ ——

A boomerang always comes back to you no matter where you throw it. My dad says he wants to invent money like that.

—— ★ ——

I bought a boomerang that came with a money-back guarantee, but every time I tried to return it, it came back to me.

—— ★ ——

A boomerang always comes back to you. It's like a yo-yo with no strings attached.

—— ★ ——

A boomerang always comes back to where it started. Boy, if I had a memory like that I might be able to pass geography.

—— ★ ——

Santa Claus gave me a boomerang for Christmas. The next day it went back to the North Pole.

—— ★ ——

You throw the boomerang as hard as you can and it winds up right back where it started. I've made golf shots like that.

—— ★ ——

The boomerang makes a complete circle and comes right back to just about where it started. It's kind of like a cab ride in a strange city.

—— ★ ——

I once had a car that was part boomerang. No matter where I drove it, it always returned to the dealer's repair shop.

—— ★ ——

My uncle crossed a boomerang with a homing pigeon. No matter where you threw it, it would return twice.

—— ★ ——

# INDEX